A RENAISSANCE CHRISTMAS

NATIONAL GALLERY OF ART

A Bulfinch Press Book • Little, Brown and Company

BOSTON • TORONTO • LONDON

First Edition

Library of Congress Cataloging-in-Publication Data

A Renaissance Christmas/National Gallery of Art.—1st ed.

p.   cm.

"A Bulfinch Press book."

Summary: Uses text from the King James Bible, selections of Renaissance poetry and carols,

and Renaissance artwork from the National Gallery to retell the Christmas story.

ISBN 0-8212-1875-1

1. Christmas in art—Juvenile literature. 2. Art, Renaissance—Juvenile literature.

3. Christmas—Juvenile literature. 4. National Gallery of Art (U.S.)—Juvenile literature.

[1. Jesus Christ—Nativity. 2. Christmas in art. 3. Art, Renaissance.]

I. National Gallery of Art (U.S.).

N8060.R4 1991

704.9'4853'09409024—dc20   91-71610

Bulfinch Press is an imprint and trademark of Little, Brown and Company (Inc.)

Published simultaneously in Canada by Little, Brown & Company (Canada) Limited

Printed in Japan

SALVATION to all that will is nigh;

That All, which always is All everywhere,

Which cannot sin, and yet all sins must bear,

Which cannot die, yet cannot choose but die,

Lo, faithful Virgin, yields Himself to lie

In prison, in thy womb; and though He there

Can take no sin, nor thou give, yet He'll wear,

Taken from thence, flesh, which death's force may try.

Ere by the spheres time was created, thou

Wast in His mind, who is thy Son, and Brother,

Whom thou conceiv'st, conceived; yea thou art now

Thy Maker's maker, and thy Father's mother;

Thou hast light in dark; and shutst in little room,

Immensity cloistered in thy dear womb.

And the angel said unto her, Fear not, Mary: for thou hast found favor with God. And, behold, thou shalt conceive in thy womb, and bring forth a son, and shalt call his name Jesus.

Then Joseph her husband, being a just man, and not willing to make her a public example, was minded to put her away privily. But while he thought on these things, behold, the angel of the Lord appeared unto him in a dream, saying, Joseph, thou son of David, fear not to take unto thee Mary thy wife: for that which is conceived in her is of the Holy Ghost.

10

*A*S *JOSEPH* was a-walking,
　　He heard an angel sing:
"This night shall be born
　　Our heavenly King.

"*H*E neither shall be born
　　In housen nor in hall,
Nor in the place of Paradise,
　　But in an ox's stall.

"*H*E neither shall be clothed
　　In purple nor in pall,
But all in fair linen
　　As wear babies all.

"*H*E neither shall be rocked
　　In silver nor in gold,
But in a wooden cradle
　　That rocks on the mould.

"*H*E neither shall be christened
　　In white wine nor red,
But with fair spring water
　　With which we were christened."

Then Joseph being raised from sleep did as the angel of the Lord had bidden him, and took unto him his wife.

Nowel, nowel, nowel, nowel, nowel, nowel!

*O*UT of youre slepe arise and wake,

For God mankind now hath itake

All of a maide without any make;

Of all women she berethe the belle.

Nowel.

*A*ND throwe a maide faire and wis

Now man is made of full grete pris;

Now angeles knelen to manes servis;

And at this time all this bifel.

Nowel.

Now all this was done,
that it might be fulfilled
which was spoken of
the Lord by the prophet,
saying, Behold, a virgin
shall be with child, and
shall bring forth a son,
and they shall call his
name Emmanuel, which
being interpreted is,
God with us.

*N*OW man is brighter than the sonne;

Now man in heven an hie shall (wonne);

Blessed be God this game is begonne

And his moder emperesse of helle.

Nowel.

16

*T*HAT ever was thralle, now is he free;

That ever was smalle, now grete is she;

Now shall God deme bothe thee and me

Unto his blisse, if we do well.

Nowel.

*N*OW man may to heven wende;

Now heven and erthe to him they bende;

He that was fo now is oure frende.

This is no nay that I you telle.

Nowel.

*N*OW blessed brother, graunte us grace,

A domes day to see thy face,

And in thy court to have a place,

That we mow there singe Nowel.

Nowel.

And it came to pass, that, when Elisabeth heard the salutation of Mary, the babe leaped in her womb; and Elisabeth was filled with the Holy Ghost. And she spake out with a loud voice, and said, Blessed art thou among women, and blessed is the fruit of thy womb.

COMFORT YE, COMFORT YE MY PEOPLE, SAITH YOUR GOD. SPEAK YE COMFORTABLY TO JERUSALEM, AND CRY UNTO HER, THAT HER WARFARE IS ACCOMPLISHED, THAT HER INIQUITY IS PARDONED: FOR SHE HATH RECEIVED OF THE LORD'S HAND DOUBLE FOR HER SINS. THE VOICE OF HIM THAT CRIETH IN THE WILDERNESS, PREPARE YE THE WAY OF THE LORD, MAKE STRAIGHT IN THE DESERT A HIGHWAY FOR OUR GOD. EVERY VALLEY SHALL BE EXALTED, AND EVERY MOUNTAIN AND HILL SHALL BE MADE LOW: AND THE CROOKED SHALL BE MADE STRAIGHT, AND THE ROUGH PLACES PLAIN: AND THE GLORY OF THE LORD SHALL BE REVEALED, AND ALL FLESH SHALL SEE IT TOGETHER: FOR THE MOUTH OF THE LORD HATH SPOKEN IT.

Now Elisabeth's full time came that she should be delivered; and she brought forth a son. And her neighbors and her cousins heard how the Lord had showed great mercy upon her; and they rejoiced with her.

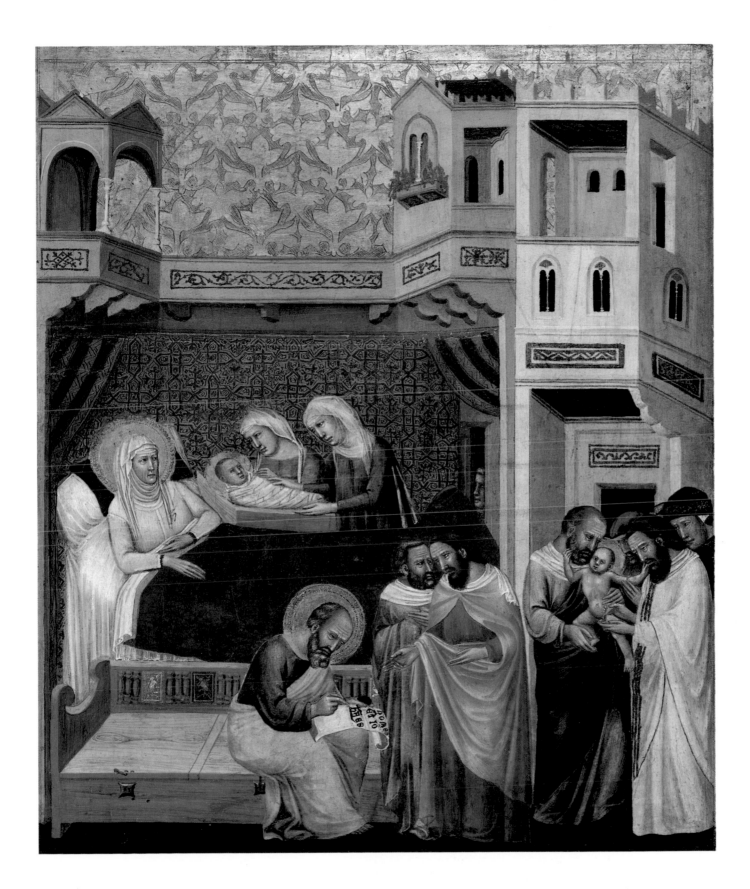

BUT THOU, BETHLEHEM EPHRATAH, THOUGH THOU BE LITTLE AMONG THE THOUSANDS OF JUDAH, YET OUT OF THEE SHALL HE COME FORTH UNTO ME THAT IS TO BE RULER IN ISRAEL; WHOSE GOINGS FORTH HAVE BEEN FROM OF OLD, FROM EVERLASTING. THEREFORE WILL HE GIVE THEM UP, UNTIL THE TIME THAT SHE WHICH TRAVAILETH HATH BROUGHT FORTH: THEN THE REMNANT OF HIS BRETHREN SHALL RETURN UNTO THE CHILDREN OF ISRAEL. AND HE SHALL STAND AND FEED IN THE STRENGTH OF THE LORD, IN THE MAJESTY OF THE NAME OF THE LORD HIS GOD; AND THEY SHALL ABIDE: FOR NOW SHALL HE BE GREAT UNTO THE ENDS OF THE EARTH. AND THIS MAN SHALL BE THE PEACE, WHEN THE ASSYRIAN SHALL COME INTO OUR LAND: AND WHEN HE SHALL TREAD IN OUR PALACES, THEN SHALL WE RAISE AGAINST HIM SEVEN SHEPHERDS, AND EIGHT PRINCIPAL MEN.

And Joseph also went up from Galilee, out of the city of Nazareth, into Judaea, unto the city of David, which is called Bethlehem (because he was of the house and lineage of David); to be taxed with Mary his espoused wife, being great with child.

*B*Y the Crib wherein reposing,
With His eyes in slumber closing
    Lay serene her Infant-boy,
Stood the beauteous mother feeling
Bliss that could not bear concealing,
    So her face o'erflowed with joy.

O THE RAPTURE naught could smother
Of the most Immaculate Mother.
    Of the sole begotten One;
When with laughing heart exulting,
She beheld her hopes resulting
    In the great birth of her Son.

*W*HO would not with jubilation
See the happy consolation
    Of Christ's Mother undefiled?
Who would not be glad surveying
Christ's dear Mother bending, praying,
    Playing with her heavenly Child?

And she brought forth her first-born son, and wrapped him in swaddling clothes, and laid him in a manger; because there was no room for them in the inn.

*F*OR a sinful world's salvation,
Christ her Son's humiliation
    She beheld and brooded o'er;
Saw Him weak, a child, a stranger,
Yet before Him in the manger
    Kings lie prostrate and adore.

O'ER that lowly manger winging,
Joyful hosts from heaven were singing
    Canticles of holy praise;
While the old man and the maiden,
Speaking naught, with hearts o'erladen,
    Pondered on God's wondrous ways.

O! CHRISTIANS! Hail the dawn,
    Your joyous tributes pay;
Its glory shines from shore to shore,
    For Christ was born this day.

O DAWN of wondrous truth—
    God of a Virgin born;
A Son who shall our souls redeem
    Is ours this Christmas morn.

And the word was made
flesh, and dwelt among us
(and we beheld his glory,
the glory as of the only
begotten of the Father),
full of grace and truth.

And there were in the same country shepherds abiding in the field, keeping watch over their flock by night. And, lo, the angel of the Lord came upon them, and the glory of the Lord shone round about them: and they were sore afraid. And the angel said unto them, Fear not: for, behold, I bring you good tidings of great joy, which shall be to all people. For unto you is born this day in the city of David a Saviour, which is Christ the Lord.

And suddenly there was with the angel a multitude of the heavenly host praising God, and saying, Glory to God in the highest, and on earth peace, good will toward men.

I SAW the curl'd drops, soft and slow,

    Come hovering o'er the place's head;

Offering their whitest sheets of snow,

    To furnish the fair Infant's bed.

Forbear, said I, be not too bold;

Your fleece is white, but 'tis too cold.

I SAW th' obsequious Seraphim

    Their rosy fleece of fire bestow,

For well they now can spare their wing,

    Since Heaven itself lies here below.

Well done, said I; but are you sure

Your down, so warm, will pass for pure?

And they came with haste, and found Mary, and Joseph, and the babe lying in a manger.

N O, NO! your King's not yet to seek

    Where to repose His royal head;

See, see, how soon His new-bloom'd cheek

    'Twixt mother's breasts is gone to bed!

Sweet choice, said we! no way but so,

Not to lie cold, yet sleep in snow.

And Mary said, My soul doth magnify the Lord, and my spirit hath rejoiced in God my Saviour. For he hath regarded the low estate of his handmaiden: for, behold, from henceforth all generations shall call me blessed.

*T*HERE is no rose of swich vertu

As is the rose that bare Jhesu.

Alleluia.

*F*OR in this rose conteined was

Hevene and erthe in litel space,

Res miranda.

*B*E that rose we may weel see

There be o God in persones three,

Pares forma.

*T*HE aungeles sungen the schepherdes to

Gloria in excelsis Deo.

Gaudeamus.

*L*EVE we all this werdly merthe,

And folwe we this joyful berthe.

Transeamus.

*T*ELL US, thou clear and heavenly tongue,

Where is the Babe but lately sprung?

Lies He the lily-banks among?

Or say, if this new Birth of ours

Sleeps, laid within some ark of flowers,

Spangled with dewlight; thou canst clear

All doubts, and manifest the where.

Declare to us, bright Star, if we shall seek

Him in the morning's blushing cheek,

Or search the beds of spices through,

To find Him out.

                Star. No, this ye need not do;

But only come and see Him rest

A Princely Babe in's mother's breast.

Now when Jesus was born in Bethlehem of Judaea in the days of Herod the king, behold, there came wise men from the east to Jerusalem, saying, Where is he that is born King of the Jews? for we have seen his star in the east, and are come to worship him.

33

He's seen, He's seen! why then a round,

Let's kiss the sweet and holy ground;

And all rejoice that we have found

A King before conception crown'd.

Come then, come then, and let us bring

Unto our pretty Twelfth-tide King,

Each one his several offering;

And when night comes we'll give Him wassailing;

And that His treble honours may be seen,

We'll choose Him King, and make His mother

Queen.

And, lo, the star, which
they saw in the east, went
before them, till it came
and stood over where the
young child was. When
they saw the star, they
rejoiced with exceeding
great joy.

*I*NSTEAD OF neat Inclosures

   Of inter-woven Osiers;

   Instead of fragrant Posies

   Of Daffadills, and Roses;

   Thy cradle, Kingly Stranger,

      As Gospell tells,

      Was nothing els,

   But, here, a homely manger.

*B*UT we with Silks, (not Cruells)

   With sundry precious Jewells,

   And Lilly-work will dresse Thee;

   And as we dispossesse thee

   Of clouts, wee'l make a chamber,

      Sweet Babe, for Thee,

      Of Ivorie,

   And plaister'd round with Amber.

And when they were come into the house, they saw the young child with Mary his mother, and fell down, and worshipped him: and when they had opened their treasures, they presented unto him gifts; gold, and frankincense, and myrrh.

38

And when eight days were accomplished for the circumcising of the child, his name was called Jesus, which was so named of the angel before he was conceived in the womb.

WHO CAN forget—never to be forgot—

The time, that all the world in slumber lies,

When, like the stars, the singing angels shot

To earth, and heaven awakèd all his eyes

To see another sun at midnight rise

On earth? Was never sight of pareil fame,

For God before man like Himself did frame,

But God Himself now like a mortal man became.

A CHILD *He was,* and had not learnt to speak,

That with His word the world before did make;

His mother's arms Him bore, He was so weak,

That with one hand the vaults of heaven could shake,

See how small room my infant Lord doth take,

Whom all the world is not enough to hold!

Who of His years, or of His age hath told?

Never such age so young, never a child so old.

And when the days of
her purification according
to the law of Moses
were accomplished,
they brought him to
Jerusalem, to present
him to the Lord.

Behold, the angel of the
Lord appeareth to Joseph
in a dream, saying,
Arise, and take the young
child and his mother, and
flee into Egypt, and be
thou there until I bring
thee word: for Herod will
seek the young child to
44   destroy him.

JESUS CHRIST of Nazareth,

    He is born of a maiden pure,

Wherein God is blessed.

ALL the angels of the kingdom of Heaven,

    And all the shepherds of earth

They sung, they had great joy.

When he arose, he took the young child and his mother by night, and departed into Egypt. And was there until the death of Herod: that it might be fulfilled which was spoken of the Lord by the prophet, saying, Out of Egypt have I called my son.

WHEN Herod became aware

    That a little child was born,

Then had he in his heart great spite.

HE had search made here and there,

    For young children of two years,

All of which he deprived of life.

WHEN our Lady heard this,

    And that Herod was thus massacring infants,

She felt in her heart great grief.

SHE spoke to Joseph without delay;

    Get you ready, we must away,

We should be gone, 'tis more than time.

*A*LL the angels of the kingdom of Heaven,

And all the clergy of the earth,

They all delighted were and glad!

*J*ESUS CHRIST of Nazareth,

He is born of a maiden pure,

Wherein God is blessed.

50

Lully, lulla, thou little tiny child;

By, by lullay, lullay, thou little tiny child;

By, by lully, lullay.

*O*SISTERS too! how may we do

For to preserve this day

This poor youngling, for whom we do sing

By, by, lully, lullay.

*H*EROD the King in his raging,

Charged he hath this day

His men of might, in his own sight,

All young children to slay.

*T*HAT woe is me, poor child for thee!

And ever morn and day,

For thy parting neither say nor sing,

By, by, lully lullay.

Then Herod, when he saw that he was mocked of the wise men, was exceeding wroth, and sent forth, and slew all the children that were in Bethlehem, and in all the coasts thereof, from two years old and under, according to the time which he had diligently enquired of the wise men.

But when Herod was
dead, behold, an angel of
the Lord appeareth in a
dream to Joseph in Egypt,
saying, Arise, and take
the young child and his
mother, and go into the
land of Israel: for they
are dead which sought
the young child's life.

54

SLEEP, my Child, in sleep recline;

Lullaby, mine Infant fair,

Heaven's King,

All glittering,

Full of grace as lilies rare.

CLOSE thine eyelids, O my treasure,

Loved past measure,

Of my soul, the Lord, the pleasure;

Lullaby, O regal Child,

On the hay

My joy I lay;

Love celestial, meek and mild.

WHY dost weep, my Babe? alas!

Cold winds that pass

Vex, or is't the little ass?

Lullaby, O Paradise;

Of my heart

Thou Saviour art;

On thy face I press a kiss.

AS I in hoary Winter's night stood shivering in the snow,

Surpris'd I was with sudden heat which made my

      heart to glow;

And lifting up a fearful eye to view what fire was near,

A pretty Babe, all burning bright, did in the air appear;

Who, scorchèd with exceeding heat, such flood of tears

      did shed,

As though His floods should quench His flames, which

      with His tears were fed.

"Alas!" quoth He, "but newly born in fiery heat I fry,

Yet none approach to warm their hearts or feel My fire but I.

And the child grew, and waxed strong in spirit, filled with wisdom: and the grace of God was upon him.

"My faultless breast the furnace is, the fuel, wounding thorns,

Love is the fire and sighs the smoke, the ashes, shames

      and scorns.

The fuel Justice layeth on and Mercy blows the coals,

The metal in this furnace wrought are men's defilèd souls,

For which, as now on fire I am to work them to their good,

So will I melt into a bath to wash them in My blood."

With this He vanish'd out of sight and swiftly shrunk away,

And straight I callèd unto mind that it was Christmas Day.

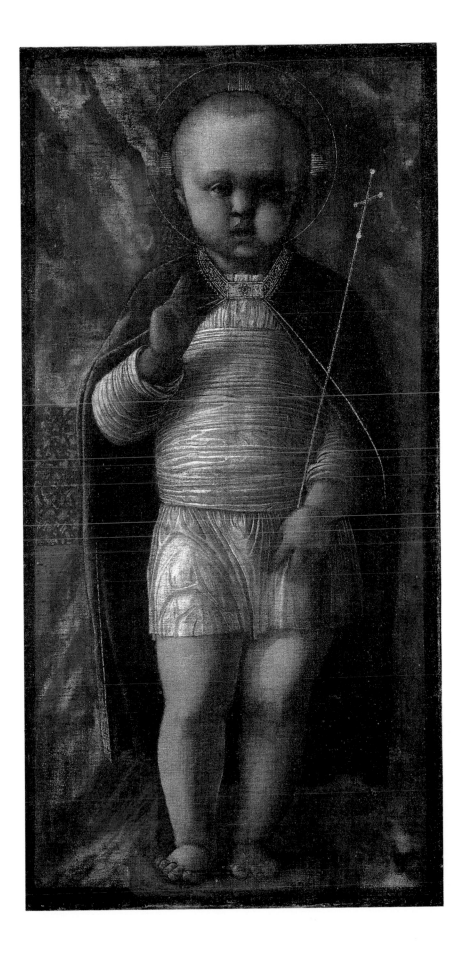

LIST OF WORKS OF ART

All works of art reproduced in A Renaissance Christmas *are in the collections of the National Gallery of Art, Washington, D.C.*

FRONT JACKET
Juan de Flandes, active 1496–1519 Hispano-Flemish
The Nativity, ca. 1508/1519
Oil and tempera on wood, 43½″ × 31¼″
Samuel H. Kress Collection 1961.9.23

BACK JACKET
Giovanni di Paolo di Grazia, ca. 1403–1482 Sienese
The Adoration of the Magi, ca. 1450
Tempera on wood, 10¼″ × 17¾″
Andrew W. Mellon Collection 1937.1.13

PAGE 4
Giovanni Bellini, ca. 1427–1516 Venetian
Madonna and Child, ca. 1475
Tempera and oil on wood, 21″ × 16¾″
Samuel H. Kress Collection 1939.1.352

PAGE 7
Giovanni di Paolo di Grazia
The Adoration of the Magi (detail)
(see description for back jacket)

PAGES 8–9
Filippo Lippi, ca. 1406–1469 Florentine
The Annunciation, probably after 1440
Wood, 40½″ × 64″
Samuel H. Kress Collection 1943.4.35

PAGE 11
Gerard David, ca. 1460–1523 Netherlandish
The Rest on the Flight into Egypt (detail), ca. 1510
Oil on oak, 16½″ × 16⅝″
Andrew W. Mellon Collection 1937.1.43

PAGE 12
Bernard van Orley, ca. 1488–1541 Netherlandish
The Marriage of the Virgin, ca. 1513
Oil on oak (?), 21⅞″ × 13⅜″
Samuel H. Kress Collection 1952.5.48

PAGE 15
Anonymous, 15th century French
The Expectant Madonna with Saint Joseph
Oil and tempera on wood, 27⅝″ × 13⅝″
Samuel H. Kress Collection 1952.5.32

PAGE 16
Piero di Cosimo, 1462–1521 Florentine
The Visitation with Saint Nicholas and Saint Anthony Abbot, ca. 1490
Oil on wood, 72½″ × 74¼″
Samuel H. Kress Collection 1939.1.361

PAGE 19
Master of the Life of Saint John the Baptist, active second quarter 14th century, School of Rimini
Scenes from the Life of Saint John the Baptist, probably ca. 1330
Tempera on wood, 19¼″ × 16″
Samuel H. Kress Collection 1952.5.68

PAGE 20
Master of the Prado "Adoration of the Magi," active probably third quarter of 15th century Netherlandish
The Presentation in the Temple (detail), ca. 1470/80
Oil on oak, 22¹³⁄₁₆″ × 18¹³⁄₁₆″
Samuel H. Kress Collection 1961.9.28

PAGE 23
Petrus Christus, active 1444–1472/73 Netherlandish
The Nativity, ca. 1450
Oil on oak, 50¼″ × 37⅜″
Andrew W. Mellon Collection 1937.1.40

PAGE 24
Filippino Lippi, ca. 1457–1504 Florentine
The Adoration of the Child, ca. 1480
Wood, 32″ × 22⅛″
Andrew W. Mellon Collection 1937.1.18

PAGE 27
Jacopo Bassano, ca. 1515–1592 Venetian
The Annunciation to the Shepherds, probably ca. 1555/60
Oil on canvas, 41¾″ × 32½″
Samuel H. Kress Collection 1939.1.126

LIST OF TEXTS

Designed by Martine Bruel

Composition: Jacket and title page in Bauer Text Initials

by the Composing Room of New England

Calligraphy by Raphael Boguslav

Text pages in Bodoni Book, Zapf Chancery Light, Demi Bold and Bold

by Hamilton Phototype

Printed and bound by Dai Nippon Printing, Tokyo